I love you
and it's not
enough

CHRISTA KATE
ANDERSON

Love is hard to find,
No one cares,
Family is just a word,
And making friends is a joke.

I love you and It's not enough is a poetry collection about life, love, family relationships, people and mental health.
It's been my way of coping with life and not-so-fortunate events. Starting from childhood up into my adulthood.

No one warns you how much harder it can get, how to survive in a world where everyone is out for themselves, especially if you don't know who you are yet and that you do matter, irrespective of what anyone else says.

The search for love and connection started when I could legally call myself an adult. I was in for a cruel and heartbreaking awakening and the realization that I'm just not ready for life. All that Mom and Dad gave me were self-doubts and the need for anyone to give me what they failed to do.

People seem to be so cold these days. It's so hard to trust anyone but yourself, and you hope that you at least have yourself to hold. I wish a lot of things were different, but so often there isn't that choice, you just scramble in the hope of coping with your past, yourself and your future.

- Christa Kate Anderson-

CONTENTS

Family

I love you and it's not enough • Christa Kate Anderson

It all started with family.
It's the years that sometimes still haunt me,
It's the memories I wish I didn't get.
People like to call it that, and it holds this meaning
That often becomes an excuse for more and more abuse.
You are expected to tolerate it.
And still care despite all that.
Well, I don't anymore,
And I don't have to force myself to do it.
I don't have a family.
It's just me now and that is ok.

Do you think you have it figured out?

I used to think you have it figured out,
And you sure did play that part well.
You think you know everything,
And act like you certainly do,
It's only your opinion and what you want.
I wanted to be like you and looked up to you.
Thinking I see freedom and strength,
When it was arrogance and blissful ignorance.
You said you know what to do,
And what is the best,
Not only for you but for everyone else.
Who cares if they don't agree with you?
They must be out of their mind,
You can't possibly be wrong,
Your ego won't allow you to be so foolish.
I know you do care about your family,
My mistake was thinking that I am part of that,
When I'm not and never came close to being.
And the past means nothing,
Pictures are proof of something that never was.
Just an illusion and life I wish I never had.
Something I want to forget.

She's not coming back

She is gone and she's not coming back.
And that is a good thing.
I just wish I could erase it
From every part of me.
I don't want to remember her face,
Or what she said,
Her memory is reduced to the part of me,
That I can't control.
It forces me to relive it again,
I don't know how to make it stop.
Or will it ever go away?
Maybe it's just a part of me,
That will stay somewhere deep inside.
It's so sad that all that is left is this,
Not a single good memory,
The words and faces are gone,
But the feeling remains.
How can it still hurt me so much?
I remind myself that it's not real.

She's just a nightmare now

I wake up, she's not real.
And I am safe.
Please make it stop and let me forget.
Until the next night when I see her again,
It all comes back.

She's just a nightmare that doesn't stop.
I'm back there with her and trying to escape.
It feels like my life is so far from me.
It's just the prison from way back then.
I'm back to counting the days,
Just now the hope is gone.

I'm there again and she is alive again,
It feels so real like she never left,
Like I never got away.
And she didn't die.
I remember my life and it's no longer mine,
Because she is alive again.

I don't want to be like you

I might look a bit like you,
Something in my smile is similar to yours.
And the colour of your eyes looking back at me.
But when I see myself, I don't want to see you,
Any part of you that could be in me.
I'm nothing like you and I don't want to be.
You had one weakness,
And you let it get the best of you,
Surrendering your voice in ignorance,
Weak and pathetic,
Bending over to anyone and anything,
For the thing you wanted the most.
I don't hate you,
But I will despise every single part of me,
That reminds me of you,
Even if it is for a little bit.

The thought of being anything like you,
Or being compared to you scares me
It makes me wish that you never existed.
I once loved you and cared about you.
And wanted you to be there for me.
You didn't reciprocate,
Not with words or actions.
Acceptance and forgiveness can be blissful,
Especially combined with fading memories.
Some day there will be so little of you in me,
That it won't matter anymore.
Even with the parts that I can't change,
I will choose to see only me.

I love you and it's not enough • *Christta Kate Anderson*

The idea of you

I cry for you, but you don't hear me.
I need your love, but you have none to give.
You take all of me, but it's not enough,
I am left with nothing,
But you still want more.

You didn't teach me to love, it's strange to me.
I don't know how to love you or myself.
Pain is what I have, but you don't like it,
Hate is what I feel and it's so unfair.

I looked for you in other people,
Trying to make myself whole.
The love I didn't get from you,
No one could replace that.

But it wasn't you that I was looking for,
Not the real you.
I wanted the idea of you that loves me,
So I can learn to love myself.

Helpless and broken,
Before I could put myself together.
To stop looking for you outside,
And find you in me.

I am good at being you.
It's not you anymore, it's me.
And all the things you couldn't be.
All I ever wanted and knew I needed.

I love you and it's not enough • Christa Kate Anderson

Hot and cold

You are so close and yet so far.
Sometimes you care and then you don't.
And I can't predict what it will be,
Will you love me today and hate me tomorrow?

You don't hear me when I talk to you,
And you don't understand.
I want to be there for you,
But it's killing me inside.

The good times we have,
Who is pretending to care,
And who really does?
When it all comes crashing down.

When you lose the human inside of you,
What is left there for me?
All you have to give is hate,
But then you turn around, pretending it's ok.

I love you and it's not enough • Christa Kate Anderson

The unbreakable bond between us,
It's a cruel joke.
And I'm not the one laughing,
Are we still alright?

I love you, but it's bad for me,
As we go around in circles,
The ups and downs,
And it's never your fault.

It's all on me,
And I am the crazy one,
The one who's not normal,
But is it really so?

You will never change,
And it hurts so bad,
I love you,
But can't be around you.

I love you and it's not enough

I love you
And it's not enough.
My love is not enough for both of us.
It doesn't work,
When you have none inside.

I love you
And it's not enough.
If there is any love in you,
It's not for me,
I'm not the one you want.
I'm just the one that's there,
That's always been there for you,
But you don't see it,
You don't even care.

I love you,
And it's not enough.
I'm someone who cares,
And can't let you go,
Someone that would do anything for you.
Someone who you would let go,
And won't even think to blink.

I love you
And it's not enough,
Not enough to make anything better.
Not enough to keep anything good,
Because what really is there?
What really was ever there?

I love you,
And it's not enough,
It can't fix the past,
Or make a better future,
It won't fill up the void I have,
It won't give me anything I need.

I love you,
And it's not enough.
I don't know what to do.
The love you can't give,
Love you can't receive.
I love you so much,
But it will never be enough.

Society and people

Society and people still make me feel sad.

I don't want to sound negative,

It's just the realism of how the world works now.

All the unfair things.

How much of it all becomes this thing of getting on with it?

Trying to make the best of the life you have.

With all the bad things that happened to you.

It's scary how the world is changing so fast.

There are all these opportunities and all the technology,

Yet still so many people are suffering.

So many means of connection,

But the loneliness is getting out of hand.

People are forgetting how to talk to each other,

So much of what they talk about now is so shallow.

Mental health issues are on the rise,

It's difficult to live and find ways of coping.

Chewing toy

Play with me I'm yours.
Chew me up and spit me out,
Take what you like and leave the rest behind.
Piece by piece,
We can see how far it can go.

Pull me apart, see what's left inside.
Your words like teeth sinking into my skin.
It feels like a game and starts so fun.
It hurts, but just a little bit,
Just the right amount.

I let you do as you please.
Until you take too much.
And I'm left with a void to fill.
You still think we are playing a game.
The game where we both lose.

I'm only worth as much as I can do for you.
I'm just a means to your satisfaction.
Just another supply for attention.
You want me to be your obedient chewing toy.
Do you see a price tag on my skin?

I love you and it's not enough • Christa Kate Anderson

You only see yourself and what you need from me.
The chewing toy doesn't get to think or feel.
You kick it to the ground,
Pull its arms and legs apart,
Step on it and take the inside stuffing out.

I'm looking at my insides ripped apart,
As I lay like an empty shell of a stuffed animal.
Then you decide to stuff it all back together.
You think I should be thankful.
And we are back to this game we play.

I'm a shell of a person.
Nothing but a used and discarded chewing toy.
The stitches don't quite keep the stuffing inside.
There is too much of it in my arms.
And not enough down to my legs.

Seaside holiday

They come for the holiday,
The fun and laughter.
For the seaside beaches,
And the long walks after it gets dark.

They come to ride the City wheel.
And see all over her,
Explore all the best parts.
They treat her like an entertainer for the night.
She takes the money
And they have fun.

They won't be staying for too long
As the novelty of her wears off,
After they have seen the longest Pier,
And it's just another thing that's there.
It's not that special anymore.

It's just another seaside holiday.
They don't want to see her,
If she's not wrapped in shiny candy paper.
And presented on a plate
With a booklet of the best places to see.
See, that's not fun anymore,
And they don't care beyond that.

She can keep the dark corners,
And all the people there.
The forgotten places and empty shops.
The rubbish on the streets,
And the filthy overpriced homes,
Because you see, the location, the seaside.
It's all about that,
And who cares,
How it is for the ones living there?

I love you and it's not enough • Christa Kate Anderson

Friend

I can be your friend, if you will be mine.
Nothing is free as we push and pull,
One text message here and *how are you?* there,
For a balance of friendship,
We pay with our care.
We share stories and dreams,
And the times from before,
I will play as long as you do too,
As long as it's fair.
Until just one of us is there.

You're so nice

Your angry face says it all,
I'm trying to keep my calm,
Keep smiling,
And being nice to you,
I already don't like you anymore,
I don't deserve the blame for that.
I'm so sorry,
The tech doesn't work as it's supposed to.
And you can't scan your rewards card.
Dear God the misery.
Is that a reason to be so mean?
And that angry look on your face?
That tone of voice?
I'm trying to sort it out,
Every second feels like an hour,
When you look at me like that.
And I don't know what to do,
All I know is to turn it off and on again.
Maybe you should restart the app on your phone.
That usually helps, doesn't it?
When it does you change up your face,
We make small talk,
About how the tech goes wrong,
And there is that fake smile,
Don't start pretending that you're so nice.

I love you and it's not enough • Christa Kate Anderson

Another face in the crowd

You could be everything to me,
While being just another face in the crowd.
For them,
The ones who don't know you,
The ones who don't care.
It doesn't matter if it's you,
Or a million other people in your place.
You're just a face that they see.
Without any particular reason,
Moments that won't ever matter.
False promises of care and friendship,
That they can't live up to.
You're just another face in the crowd,
That they will soon forget.

It's only me and what I want

It's only me and what I want.
I am right and you are wrong.
I say I care when I don't,
It's just a game and I play pretend.
It's just the way it works.
Same words, same lies but different faces.
Remember that caring comes with a cost.
It's not what you give,
That you will get back.
And time means nothing,
It's only here and now.
I was there and now I am not,
It's like you don't know me at all.
Where was the lie?
And why do you still care?

#Lol

It's #*lol*
When we aren't even laughing.
We still crave human connection,
In a world where it's losing its meaning.
It's now *yolo* until the day we die.

Where did the real dates get lost?
#*Netflixandchill*
And the real conversations,
Well, who knows,
How to still talk beyond
This *yes* and *no*,
Hold on for a moment longer,
You will get a bonus *maybe* as well.
And it won't matter at all.

I wonder what happens
After the pleasantries are over.
No one knows how to talk,
And no one cares enough to try.

I love you and it's not enough • *Christa Kate Anderson*

We exchange short messages
And show our emotions with a bunch of emojis,
It's too difficult to use words to explain how we feel.

It's like it's this thing there,
Like so difficult to say,
But you get what I mean, like, right?
Like this is the world we live in now.
And that *like* just got annoying too fast.

But what can we ask
From a world of short attention spans,
And even shorter patience.
If you can't keep their attention,
It's not worth it if it's not catchy enough.
#inspirational

I love you and it's not enough • *Christa Kate Anderson*

Devices

You rely on your devices,
Like your life depends on it,
Like there isn't another way of life.
If anything goes wrong with tech,
It's the biggest misfortune of them all.
You are so dependent.
It's crucial for survival,
For entertainment and learning,
And to keep things running.
There is an app for everything.
One to wake you up,
You can't be trusted to do it yourself.
Another one is to get the daily steps in.
One for counting your calories,
Dear God don't go over the limit,
And a traffic light system to guide you.
Another one for keeping up with events,
Work shifts,
And appointments.
What would life be without it?
Another app to determine your happiness.

Breathe

Breathe and hold it together,
When it feels like you could scream.
It's overwhelming and loud.
And there is no way out,
They want something from you
And it's not their fault.
You are having a bad day or week,
Or month.
I know we all struggle,
But it's still so hard to be kind.
When the words of a stranger
Can make you break down,
Only kindness is nowhere to be found.

One less crappy person

If other people behave in a certain way,
That doesn't mean you have to do the same,
They are doing these little crappy things,
That isn't really a crime
But still not very nice.
The lack of thought about others,
Their convenience,
And selfishly careless nature.
Because why should you care?
Why should you think about it?
No one does.
I think that's the problem,
No one thinks about it,
No one cares.
And the cycle of these little crappy things continues.
It's the trash left on the streets and tables,
Like they don't see the bin nearby,
But if they do,
An unfinished drink goes in there for sure.
No one cares about that somebody,
That will have to change that bin,
As long as it won't be them.
It's not their problem,
Not their concern.

Words and faces

You forget the words and faces,
As time goes by.
You are happy and moving on,
But the feeling remains.
The memory of pain.

Just to come back and haunt you,
When something acts as a trigger.
It puts you back in that place,
And you wish for it to go away.
The memory of pain.

You wish to forget it ever existed,
Remembering is reliving it again.
You thought you could stop it.
It hurts the same every time.
The memory of pain.

Learning to control it.
You have to let go and live in the now.
Maybe your mind will stop the torture,
And you will forget it one day.
The memory of pain.

What doesn't kill you makes you stronger

They say,
What doesn't kill you makes you stronger.
But what if it doesn't?
What if it just breaks you?
Be grateful for all the trauma that comes your way,
Because it's making you stronger.
You don't feel stronger,
You feel lost and broken,
And you question why you need to live at all.

It's that odd thing they say,
When you have shared too much,
And there are no other words to say,
It's just too hard to admit,
That something was too messed up.
So they quickly brush it over.
What doesn't kill you, makes you stronger,
Right?

But what if it doesn't?
What if it gives you nightmares and scares you,
And you can't get rid of the memories,
The voices that keep telling you all the bad things.
What if it leaves you too broken to function?

Feeling like life is too much to handle.
Everything feels so much and too much.
And it never stops.
But just keep going,
You will get to the other side!

Well, a lot of people don't get there.
And how can we blame them for that?
The feeling of needing it all to stop,
The pain is too much to hold.
We call it a tragedy and it truly is.
With a lot of pain, suffering and questioning.

I love you and it's not enough • Christa Kate Anderson

Tool for control

Love is a tool for control in your hands.
Using it to give,
And then take it away.
Because you want to,
And it suits you.
This push-and-pull of power and attention,
You have to be the one to win.
You use it against me again.
When you decide I deserve it,
And then I don't.
Nothing happened,
Yet everything changed.

Let's play pretend

Let's play pretend,
Look how well it's working out.
It's what I need to be,
And what I need to do,
Because it's supposed to be this kind of way.

I'm trying to make it look genuine,
It's not easy to do.
And it's taking a bit of practice,
When I don't want to.

What I want doesn't matter.
I have to be what they want to see,
Playing this game,
And feeling how I'm pretending,
I hope that it looks like I'm happy.

Looking at myself from the outside,
I know it's me and I'm there.
But it doesn't feel real,
I could be anywhere else instead.
Focus on what could bring me back,
And make it real again.

You change your mind

You change your mind,
As quickly as the weather turns
From sunshine to cold rain,
It's unpredictable,
And it's unpleasant.
It's hitting me in the face,
I can't see without my glasses,
Now they are full of drops of rain.

You change your mind.
Like wind changes direction,
Now it's suddenly in my face,
It wasn't there a second ago,
And now that's all I can hear.
I can't hear myself think,
I can't see anything either.
My eyes hurt,
And it's got too overwhelming.

I love you and it's not enough • Christa Kate Anderson

You change your mind,
And you don't even know why,
Like the rainbow after a storm of rain,
It's like it didn't even happen,
And the sunshine is back again.
Only the puddles remain,
Be careful and don't step in them.

You and me

You are me and I am you,
We can be different,
But still have things to share,
Being alone and lonely are not the same.
I need you to be with me as I am with you,
So I could call you my friend.

Or is this friendship just an illusion?
Such a cruel distraction,
Where we can use each other for the time being,
Or you can use me,
When bored and in need of entertainment.
Until it's over and the next one comes along.

Disposable and easily replaceable.
I just wish you could tell me,
Or give me a warning when it changes.
If you could explain what happened.
But you won't and it's silly to want that.

I am you and you are me,
It's giving and taking as long as it's fair.
Then you come back as if nothing happened.
Or it's some sort of *sorry*,
And we are back to it until you do it again.

People

Can I tell you something?
Humans and people really aren't the same.
Business is the new morality.
And money is the King.
Let's put a price tag on human life.
See how much is worth dying for.
Where money equals worth,
We live to make as much as possible,
And it's never enough.
There is barely any time to live at all.
And it will never end until the day we die.

Lessons

You have to keep going through things,
So you can learn the lessons.
Lesson learned,
The world is evil,
You don't understand why you're here,
What is your purpose?
And why it feels like you are destined to suffer?

Things keep going in the wrong direction,
And humanity is lost in arrogance and greed.
You can't trust anyone,
And everyone is out for themselves.
Don't try to give away too much of yourself,
That will be thrown back in your face.

The world is so cold and you need to adapt.
Don't be too soft,
That will get you burned.
And don't try to be too nice,
That won't help you survive,
It's using each other until there is nothing left to take.
Build the walls around your mind and space,
Just to keep yourself safe.

And the delusion that people want to live in,
Where everything works out
And people can be your friends.
Yeah, that's not real,
That's just something they want to see,
It's hard to cope with reality.

So the picture is painted so bright and nice,
Just a shame that it's all a lie.
And they still want to force you to believe in that.
You need help coping with the brutal reality.
But who cares about that?

Boxes

Everything fits in these tight little boxes,
Don't try to step out of the lines.
That's not what is right,
Let's call it a crime.
Who cares what you want?
You do as you are told,
Power comes first and you don't complain.
You squeeze in there tight,
And don't take up too much space.
You choose your label and pick your box.
It's not a prison if freedom is an illusion.
But you thought you had a choice,
And maybe some options and more time.
Doesn't it feel good to belong?
Even if you can't hear yourself think.
What if they lie when they say they care?
The walls are getting too close,
And it's so difficult to breathe.
No one knows how to escape.
They call it the way of life and order.
You run around in circles and get nowhere.

I love you and it's not enough • Christa Kate Anderson

Customer service

It's the smile
When saying *Hi, how are you?*
And *what will it be for you today?*

For some people,
It will be their only interaction for the day.
With a real person in the real world.

Not hiding behind a screen,
And I know it takes a lot for some to do it.
So it's nice to be noticed,
Greeted with a smile and warm welcome.

It's not only selling coffee,
I think they could be on to something,
When they say it's these moments as well,
And making them count.

It's a little bit of rare kindness,
That we can share between us.
Even if it's making just a moment for someone
A little bit more bearable.
It's still better than nothing at all.

Between all the rushing,
The state of hurry just to get it all done,
A little bit of slowing it down helps.
And it doesn't cost anything to be kind.

Fake smiles and faces

We hide behind fake smiles and faces,
The humour and jokes, and saying: *I'm doing ok.*
Talking so much and so loud,
Not saying what we want to.

Just to be heard amongst the people,
Who don't want to listen.
We are real when no one is looking,
The fear of being too much,
No one wants to show their true self anymore.

Are we so delusional to think that they care?
As they pretend to listen and call you their friend,
Do we know what they mean?
We should rethink what this is.

So many times we've been unbearable,
Shamed and judged for showing something real.
Then we stopped trying,
They simply can't and won't understand.
And why would they care?

Loneliness is satisfied with fun and laughter,
Boredom with someone who can entertain,
And caring is a selective privilege,
That's not for everyone.

I love you and it's not enough • Christa Kate Anderson

1 in 6 people

She said that it is one in six people,
That one will be the unkind one,
The difficult one,
The one that just woke up today,
And decided to get into an argument,
For no apparent reason,
Maybe he enjoys the thrill,
Who knows?
The world definitely revolves around him.
How dare anything not go his way?
Has the universe gone mad today?
And some silly little cashier
Is the perfect opportunity to assert his dominance,
And prove his point,
And make the whole place know
How angry and upset he is.
The silly little sorry won't cut it this time,
For the sorry isn't enough,
Not enough attention,
Not enough of making a fuss,
Not enough for everyone to know,
How important he is.
And how sorry they all really should be.

Good or bad

Someone once told me,
That people aren't good or bad.
And I shouldn't be judging them as such.
The difference between a person and their behaviour.
It's their behaviour that can be one or the other,
It's so easy to put that label on yourself and others.
We want to be good, right?
But what does that mean,
As nothing is purely good or bad?
And who has the definitions for them both?
There can be reasons for bad behaviour,
But it doesn't make it right and is not an excuse for it.
Imagine a child being told,
They were bad for misbehaving,
Were they bad or was their behaviour bad?

Pretending to care

The biggest lie to tell is to yourself,
Saying that you care,
When you don't.
Not knowing the difference,
Because that's not what a good person does,
And you are a good person, right?

Or it's just an idea,
And you so desperately want it to be true?
You would rather get mad at someone in need of help.
Lying to yourself and others,
Why don't you tell me the truth?
And most importantly to yourself.

Tell me how it is for you,
And that you don't want to see,
What you perceive as negativity,
Because it's not in line with your idea of the world.
And you simply don't care,
That's real and raw,
And better than pretending to be good,
I would respect you for being honest.

I love you and it's not enough • Christa Kate Anderson

The truth, dream and reality

Stand up, sit down and look to the left,
And now to the right.
There you go, the perfect picture,
The truth, the dream, and your reality,
What more could there be?

You're welcome, I know what's for the best.
I know what you want and what you need,
And I am never wrong, my way is the right way.
If you dare to question me,
I will show you hell, but only because I care.

You did it? Well done, good job.
And now smile, say: Thank *you*, and bow to me.
Are you happy now?
I'm sure you are,
No is not an answer,
Please nod your head and pretend.

Oh, are you saying no?
Wow, good luck to you!
You think you have the freedom of choice,
That's so funny to me,
Are you ready to be the odd one out?
The only good choice is me and you know it.

I don't want you to suffer.
Do you have what it takes?
You will see what you want to see,
Within and out,
That's how I made you,
You can't fight me.

Please stop lying to yourself,
And come back to your senses.
Still no?
Oh well, this is on you now,
You go and survive without me.
I will make sure you are sorry.

When you will question,
What is right and wrong,
Yourself and others,
Crying alone in the dark.
You will be back to me crawling on your knees,
So I can give you your truth, dream, and reality.

I love you and it's not enough • Christa Kate Anderson

Customer policy

It's not my fault,
I didn't make the rules that you don't like.
Yet there you are looking at me
Like it's my personal failure,
Like I owe you some explanation,
Like I decided to ruin your day.
And you don't take my apology,
(I shouldn't be saying sorry).
I'm saying sorry over and over again.
That's not enough for you to stop,
The best way is to just let you do it,
Apologise some more,
Then get on with my day as if nothing happened.
And keep smiling for the person after you.

The Handbook of a Narcissist

You have to think that your needs come first.
Always.
And no exceptions.
Your opinions are facts,
And they are always right.
Your struggles and suffering mean the most.
Make sure the attention is always on you,
It doesn't matter what the subject is,
Make sure to bring it back to you.
Make sure people like you,
Well, how could they not?
You are absolutely brilliant.
At all that you are and do.
Naturally.
You don't care what anyone thinks,
Or whose feelings you might hurt.
They don't matter at all,
Only you matter and they don't.
And don't break the rules for anyone.
Be it your friend or mother, or son,
It doesn't matter.
They don't matter.
The only thing that will ever matter is you.

City Centre

This God-awful place!
I can't believe it,
I have to come here again.
The people annoying me,
Their presence - so loud,
Please, let me out.

The streets are full and busy,
And they talk over each other,
It all becomes this blob of mixed sounds.
Wherever I look,
Someone is talking, banging and shouting.
And the road needs to be fixed again.

Some of them try to talk to me,
Sell me something,
Get me to look at something they have,
Get something out of me,
My attention, time and my money,
If I have any to spare.

I love you and it's not enough • Christa Kate Anderson

And don't be rude,
Don't walk away.
You owe them this moment in time.
Because they looked at you,
And thought you are next.

Some of them intrude with their noise,
And call it showing their voice.
I don't want to hear it,
It's never any good.
Yet, it's still there.

I'm still there,
And I want to go home,
That's enough of it for the day.
Until I will have to come out again.

I love you and it's not enough • Christa Kate Anderson

Shitway

Welcome to Shitway
Can I take your order?
What can I get for you today?
And how is your day going?
Ohh, wait,
I don't care,
Get lost, go away!
I really don't like you or anyone else here.
I'm overworked, stressed out,
And quite angry,
Sorry, it's not personal,
It's so hard to keep pretending.
Yet another night when I couldn't sleep,
When the day before was so exhausting.
The place is just a mess from both ends.
The workload just keeps increasing.
Another day,
We are short of a person or two.
Again.
It's always something that goes wrong.
And everyone here hates it,
Everyone talks about leaving,
And they do as soon as they can.

68

I love you and it's not enough • Christa Kate Anderson

But let's try and shut it up with some positivity.
And keep pretending a little longer,
Let's fool the new guy for a while,
Let's trap the new girl,
And tell her it's all so good in here.
Positive vibes only,
Don't bring in negativity,
Don't tell them how it feels working here,
Let them find out for themselves.
They are in for quite the surprise,
We can't spoil the fun of that.
So you can get your sandwich
With a side of resentment
And a forced smile,
From underpaid and overtired workers,
Who are just trying to tolerate you,
As you feel like an extra burden,
In between all the cleaning jobs.
And have a good day,
But please don't come back.

Monsters

He's hiding away his monster,
He lives under their bed.
And asks for a place to stay.

He moved in one day unannounced,
And now refuses to go away.
It's his home now,
And he will become their friend.

She's hiding away her monster
She lives under their bed.
She moved in one day unannounced,
It's her home now,
And she refuses to go away.

She's not friends with his monster,
They don't know how to play.
Both of them want to get their own way.

It's screaming in millions of voices
And fingernails scraping the floor.
No one wants to leave,
And they both can't stay.

Victim

Cold blood is her badge of honour,
As he lies on the bedroom floor.
She can't be fooled anymore.
He definitely had it coming,
And she's the perfect victim.
Her dark and twisted locks
Wrapped around his neck.
But it's never her fault.
She's got the voice of pain.
And he kept falling for it,
Like she's something he will save.
She didn't need saving,
Just someone who wouldn't lie,
But he just had this craving.
Of another that didn't die.

Perfect reality

Words bleed out the truth,
That they don't want to see.
They are covering it up with stories of fairytales.

It's easier that way,
Because who wants to hear the truth,
When it's something they don't like.
And they don't want to hear,
Hell, they even will go so far,
As create their perfect little reality.

Where everything fits,
Everything works out.
At least for them,
And don't mind the other ones,
We aren't them,
We don't belong.
And they don't care at all.

Everything is built upon power,
And pretending,
Well, pretending that they care,
And they will say that they do.
They have to,
To keep this show going.

Love

The story of us lives on in these pages.
You know I love our pictures,
And I love the words as well.
As we learn about what all of this means.
And how to be there for each other,
You are still the one I want and love.

Double the happy and double the pain

Double the happy and double the pain,
When it's shared, it feels like my own.
I knew that it would come to this,
But I'm still surprised.

I just wish to see you happy and better,
But it's not always the case,
And I hate that I can't take your pain away,
It hurts and feels worse on so many levels.

It's a mirror up in my heart,
It hurts more because of something you're going through,
Or something that happened to you.
I can do my best to be there and try to make it better.

Anything you need me to do and be.
And I hope that you will let me,
As I don't want to see the day,
When I can't make sure you are doing okay.

This is the part where I know I love you,
For what kind of person you are,
Just being you and true to yourself.
I want the best for you whatever it may be,
As long as you are happy.

I love you and it's not enough • *Christa Kate Anderson*

With you

I love myself when I am with you,
Nothing is too much or too little.
You bring out the best of me,
And I'm not scared of showing you the bad.

I missed you so much before,
When I didn't know what I was missing,
I wish you were there,
When I pushed in pieces that didn't fit in.

Hurting myself in the process,
Trying so hard for something so wrong,
And having nothing to show for it,
But pain and destruction.

I don't have to think anymore,
It's just me and you,
And it feels so easy and free.
From day one to now and tomorrow.

I love you and it's not enough • Christa Kate Anderson

Getting to know you

I want to know what you know,
To feel what you feel,
You can show me,
How it is to be you,
What makes you tick and how you think?

Tell me what excites you and show me why.
I will love to see what makes you happy,
And feel that with you.
I want you to be you.

Tell me what hurts you the most,
I want this to be real,
And you don't have to hide.
I'm not saying that it's easy,
Just that it's worth it.

I have to let you figure it out,
And trust that you can.
As I do with myself,
You can trust me that I can.

I love you and it's not enough • Christa Kate Anderson

When my first instinct is to try and help,
But I can't.
Not fully and it's out of my control.
The things that hurt you.
I can't win.

That won't stop me from trying,
As much as I want you.
All of who you are and will be.
And all the things that made you.

Love language

I need your presence to feel alive.
And your body against mine.
My hand in your hair pulling you closer,
A kiss that could go on forever.

I need your touch to feel loved.
The way you put your arms around me,
And make me feel safe.
The feeling of your body,
Your kisses on my neck.

My head on your chest and arms around you.
Nothing compares to sleeping as you hold me.
When it feels like time stops.
And nothing else matters.

Your eyes and the way you smile.
Having you near me feels like home.
And the safety and comfort of hearing you breathe,
As you sleep next to me.

I love you and it's not enough • Christa Kate Anderson

It's You

It's the taste of your favourite chocolates.
It's the feeling of your voice,
And the sound of your breath.
It's the way you feel like peace,
After a very long day.
Your hugs are magic,
And make everything better.
Your kindness and strength,
And that very short temper.
It's the healthy flippancy
And sarcasm that lives in your mind.
It's how you're the only thing that's right.

The meaning

When you say that you love him,
Have you thought about what it means?
The feeling itself and actions that follow?

Saying that you will know sounds like a cruel joke.
Because, what if you don't?
And it takes you a few tries to get to that.

Is it him or something he does
And how it makes you feel?
The fact of making it about you,
Using him as a mirror to see something you don't.

The idea of him that you have,
Or the real person in front of you?
It can be hard to tell the difference.
Would it still be there if you took yourself out of the picture?

He is mine

He doesn't like loud places
And noise,
But he does like my voice.
He hates all people and their ways,
But he loves me.
I'm his exception to the rule of crappy people.
And he is mine.

The best thing

You look for the very best thing,
The one that feels right and fits,
But can you measure up,
And be all that you require?

Can't be asking for something you can't provide,
It simply isn't fair,
And no one should be treated like that.
Between all the lists and checkmarks.

Make sure you meet them yourself,
As the best of self-reflection has its limits,
And your ego asks questions.

It shouldn't be too hard to decide.
If he is the best you can do.
And are you the best you?

I miss you

I miss you and I miss us,
How we could talk before,
How I could tell you everything.
Now I don't think I can or even want to.
I wish I could.
I wish it could still be ok.
But I am tired and I am hurt,
Does it matter that I'm spending my nights crying?
Or how bad it hurts, how much I worry?
And I can't shut it off,
I can't do what seems to be logical because it doesn't feel right.
And I never meant to hurt you,
I am sorry and I feel bad that I did.
But you do it all the time.
It's just always me saying that it's ok and it's fine.
Trying to understand you, wait and be patient,
I want to trust that it would be ok.
I want us to work so badly but it is making me so unhappy.
And I'm trying to hide it and be strong.
But then nothing seems right and I miss us already.
It's only been a few days,
I'm trying to get through the days.
Now I wish I had more time with you,
Maybe I would remember it more then,
And more pictures with you, anything really.

Invite me in

Your mind works so differently,
I wish you would invite me in.
It's like this little world of yours.
That's only for you,
Where no one else is allowed.

If you wish to invite me in,
I'll have to be respectful.
It would be amazing to be in your head,
To be so close to you for a moment.
To feel like you for a day.

If you invite me in.
You could finally show me,
All of those things,
Where your words are lacking.
And all of your ways,
That you can't explain.

I love you and it's not enough • *Christa Kate Anderson*

If you invite me in,
We can leave out the shoes,
I'd get to know your inner voice,
Find out what it says to you,
I hope it won't be making too much noise.

If you invite me in,
I'd love to make use of all of your senses.
I could see with your eyes,
Feel with your skin,
And hear the world as you do.
Only then I would have a clue,
About how it feels to be you.

I love you and it's not enough • *Christa Kate Anderson*

One of a kind

He likes mint chocolate,
But not mint tea,
It's green tea with honey,
He's eating the grapes in size order.
Trying to count out the peas,
(That proves to be impossible).
He's looking for the perfect size,
The perfect texture of tomatoes,
He is cleaning anything he wants to touch.
(Please don't touch it afterwards).
He is really my one-of-a-kind person,
That's all mine.

I love you and it's not enough • Christa Kate Anderson

Guitar

He loves the sound of his favourite guitar.
He is treating her well.
And knows how to play with her strings.
She's getting his attention now,
But she's not the only one he loves.
The other ones,
They are in his bedroom,
And in the living room as well.
Two of them by his night table,
One next to him in the bed.
As much as his house is full,
And mind consumed with her melody,
He's on the lookout for more.
Another new love to add to his collection,
Another one,
As he looks for the purple one.
She will be the one that's special.
People can tell him he's mad,
And that he's running out of space.
But what good would that do?
As he couldn't care less.

The random tomato

He said it isn't a vegetable,
It's a fruit!
And he puts it in a fruit salad.
Well, I think it's just grapes,
Raisins and cheese there,
But still the tomato there is so random.
Like it doesn't know where it belongs.
But he doesn't care about any of that,
He just slices it up
In that particular way,
Four.
Always four.
Each slice gets cut into four pieces.
And it's right,
And it makes sense.
And the world goes on for another day.

Self-image

Look pretty

Look pretty,
You know that you can.
It's not that hard to put on a face.
And show them that smile.
Who cares as long as they believe,
And leave you alone.

Look pretty because they think it matters.
It's what they want to see,
Why don't you show them?
They don't want the real thing,
Just close enough will do.

It will be so easy to trick them,
They will see what they want to see.
And move on thinking that it's all ok,
With a false sense of thinking that they care.

Beautiful

Beautiful.
It's not what they want you to be.
Look in the mirror and tell me,
That you like what you see.

If it's too hard, then tell me why,
And who told you so?
It's not your voice,
That wants to criticize.

The way they want to see you,
It's not how you see yourself.
And it's hard to play pretend.
Can you learn to like what you see?

I used to like my pictures

I used to like taking pictures of myself,
The old ones feel more like me.
Not this one here and now,
This feels like some in-between version of something to come.
I've been there before and it's back again.
It's just dragging out for too long.
And it's so hard to care,
Allowing emotion means I can't function.
Let me just stay in bed and cry.
If only that would help,
It just gives me a headache.
Why does it always feel like I'm worth less,
If I don't like how I look?
Do others see me the same way?
It's trying so hard not to hate it,
I'm trying to cope and not take pictures,
Because that's a reminder.
It feels like I'm failing so hard,
And it's not only how I look and feel.
Everything else is falling apart as well.
What used to be normal,
Now seems like the biggest struggle.
And I can't seem to have any compassion for myself,
Not how I would be with others.

Silent cry

Food is her reward,
The only one she's got,
The only pleasure there is.
It's also her punishment.
For getting so out of shape.
The mirror isn't her friend anymore.
It shows her someone she can't recognize.
She's looking at her flaws.
Her smile is just a cover for the silent cry.
You don't deserve to eat today.
She can't keep eating the pain away.

Hide me

I need something to hide me,
To make me feel safe.
I will grab my bag
And put it on my lap.
I'm holding my things close,
But it's more for having it there,
Something that's in front of me.
That makes me feel safe.
It's this force of habit.
That hides me a little bit,
In case it feels like anyone is looking,
I don't think they really are,
But I can't help it,
Can't help the feeling that I have to hide it.
Like it's a secret,
And no one should know,
But they already do.
Be it my jacket,
Or a pillow that I see nearby.
Anything I can keep close to me.
Anything will do,
Because I feel like I need to hide.

Good enough

I didn't know,
How good something was,
While I had it,
When I was living in that body.
And it was me and I didn't hate it.

Back then it didn't seem good enough,
And now I wish I could get it back,
Now, when everything is so much worse,
And I'm further away from what I wanted.

It feels like this backwards way of living,
One step forward and three steps back,
No, not just three,
I walked a mile back.

Now I'm stuck in being behind,
I'm falling apart,
It's not what I wanted,
Not what the goal was,
What the plan was,
Where I don't feel so bad,
And allow for a bit of peace.
Dare I say a bit of happiness?
Or at least a break from hating it.

Now I can't have it,
I can't get out of my mind,
Can't stop feeling how my body feels.
And what I think about it,
What others must be thinking about it?

Being alive

Some things are meant to be felt

It's how we always try to use words to explain,
But some things don't work like that,
There aren't enough words to say,
For it to be enough.
Some things are meant to be felt.
Getting out of my mind and into my body,
To stop all the thinking for a second,
And letting go of all the fear and worry,
So I could let myself just be here and now.
Feeling myself in the present moment,
That beautiful part of shutting it all off,
And letting that deeper part of me out.

What am I searching for?

From one moment to the next,
What am I searching for?
There's always another thing to do.
A point of focus for the mind.
Something productive or a distraction.

The feeling of guilt and disappointment,
If it's not in line with my perception of useful.
I'd love to let it go and take it as it is,
But my time is limited and irreversible,
And I have the next thing on my mind.

Can I be in the moment of doing something?
The acceptance of how it is and what it is,
And thinking of it as a thing of value.
Without the pressure of the next thing,
Finally, some peace and contentment.

Stuck

I feel like I'm stuck.
Between having so much time,
And not knowing what to do with it.
Wanting to do so much,
And then nothing at all.

I feel like I'm stuck.
Between all the things I need to do
And all the things I want to do.
I can't seem to slow down and breathe,
Before it feels like I'm falling behind.

I feel like I'm stuck.
Between who I am,
And who I want to be.
I miss the old me,
But she's not coming back.

I feel like I'm stuck.
Between everything that is there,
And all the things that I still need.
It's not getting any better,
And I'm not getting any stronger.

I feel like I'm stuck.
Between the now,
And that one day.
It feels like time is running out,
Just not fast enough.

Adult

Be an adult and do the right thing,
Did I miss out on the guide for that?
Be responsible and dependable.
People are relying on you.

And you are being watched and judged.
Society needs you to be useful,
No one likes to know they are a burden.
You know it's useful,
If it makes a profit and has a price tag.

Don't be so childish,
That's not a good look.
Be loyal but don't expect the same back,
Rules of morality are bendable.

And lying is a must-have tool.
It depends on the side of the story,
And who you are asking.
It's the joy of being an adult.

The idea of me

There is this idea of me, but it's not complete,
It's still changing,
I don't know what to do with it.
Am I doing enough and being enough of a person?

I'm tired of taking care of myself,
Feeling the emotions and crying alone.
But it's fine as long as it's just me,
There is no other way for it.

I'm tired of being strong.
I'm trying so hard,
But still, it doesn't seem to be enough,
Just enough for who, and who said it?

What is missing,
And why I'm not allowing myself to be happy?
If it's my beliefs and limitations,
Of what I think is right and wrong,
Then I have myself to blame.

Dear me

Can we play nice for once?
I would love to hate this part of you,
When you drag it down,
And push it until it breaks.

I'm here for you and it's always the same,
I know what you want and what you need,
And now it's just to feel.
It's so cruel and we are back to it again.

You know, I want to understand,
All you need is to be safe.
I'm sorry when you're not.
And can't blame you for reacting.

You showed me everything there is.
And if I let you feel,
Whatever it needs to be,
We can be at peace again.

Feelings

I am one with the dark, the lonely and the painful,
The shameful and lovely, feeling it deep within.
I wish the switch to turn off humanity was real,
Then all of this would end and we could live forever.

But we are living in the wrong universe,
For this to be so simple.
Alcohol and drugs can numb the ability to feel.
They can shut it off when it gets too much.

It didn't work out so well for them,
And I'm not the one to take the easy way out.
Not anymore,
So here it goes and I surrender.

I don't have a choice,
I feel all of it with every part of me.
From the pain that makes me want to die,
To the love that makes me wish I never would.

There is no in-between,
And they both will make me cry.
So I take it as it comes, from one day to another.
Fooling myself, that I have it figured out.

I'm tired

I'm tired of life, of trying and being and living.
It takes too much effort,
So many things seem so dull and meaningless.
I can't seem to find the point in doing anything.
It still hurts,
That I won't and can't have so many of the things
I would have wanted.

The way my life has been is too much to take.
And I would rather have nothing,
Not exist at all.
I'm stuck with a life I didn't ask for,
And wouldn't wish on anyone.

I love you and it's not enough • *Christa Kate Anderson*

I wish I wasn't born,
Then it wouldn't hurt.
We can't comprehend the idea of not being.
Nothing will happen and erase everything.
What is the point of small moments of happiness,
That is mixed with suffering,
Life and the way the world is now?

It's hard to find things that make me feel something,
Anything worth holding on to.
I wish so many things were different.
Reality is what it is for everyone.
Everyone is doing what they can,
With who they are and what they have.

There is happiness in sadness

There is happiness in sadness,
As the pain goes through you.
You let it be there,
And take it all in.
It's not there to stay,
But it seems like it will.
When all you can feel is dark,
And you wish to be numb.
It serves its purpose.
You know it's real,
And it means you can feel.
It can be there for a while,
To teach you the lesson,
Of what it means to be alive.

Acceptance

I am having a hard time accepting what is,
If it's not exactly what I want it to be,
Maybe not exactly,
I know perfect doesn't exist.
It scares me,
How unpredictable everything can be.
Is there safety in knowing that I can handle things?
I'm tired and it's been so many things already.
I wish it would be enough, but life goes on and things happen.
Could I handle even more?
I can only be what I already am.
Everything else is just learning and growing and trying.
It's not that I don't like myself,
I do and there are good things and I can be happy at times,
Not all the time, but I am trying.
I still have to learn more about myself,
What I want and need,
And what I can do to get there.
I'm not sure,
I can't plan what will happen,
I don't know what will happen.
We have just the day that's there.
The past can't be changed.
And we don't know the future.
That scares me.

Welcome to adulthood!

Welcome to adulthood!
I'm so glad you are tuning in,
You surely are in for a treat with this one,
I can promise you that.
It will be the ride of your life.

Let's start with a taste of freedom,
That's what you were hoping for.
No one to tell you to do the chores,
And your homework.

How great is that?
Chose something you can do as a job.
Now you got bills and need the money.
But who knows if you really can?
Let's waste some time with that,
To figure out you can't do that thing at all!

Welcome to adulthood!
We have jobs that drain the life out of you,
Ask for half of your soul,
And think you will sell it at discount.
Just the bare minimum will do,
The bare minimum pay,
For the bare minimum work,
To not get yourself fired.

Welcome to adulthood!
May I interest you in some anxiety?
It comes as a bonus for trying to keep yourself alive.
It's proving to be quite the challenge,
Between all the worrying, shame and self-loathing.

Welcome to adulthood!
May I offer depression at a discount as well?
Let's say a special two-for-one deal.
It can get scary and lonely here.
And other people aren't so kind.
But everyone still wants to grow up so fast.

I love you and it's not enough • Christa Kate Anderson

Mind's eye

I wonder what it's like,
How it would feel to close my eyes,
And see something.
All I have is this endless blackness,
And the faceless shapes of light blobs.

I promise it's not a lack of practice.
Who knew that picturing anything is real?
All of the things I would imagine,
The memories I could keep for longer.
People's faces, the ones I like to keep.

The nostalgic places that I can't recall.
It's like being blindfolded,
With a bad voice description,
It's also missing half of the things,
And the wifi keeps shutting down.

I love you and it's not enough • *Christa Kate Anderson*

I'm trying to remember the feeling instead.
The picture is non-existent.
My voice isn't enough to make it real.
I truly live my moments once,
I can't rewind the video,
I can't push play again.

I burn my bridges,
When I get rid of the photographs.
If I can't see it,
It might as well not exist to me.
It's a useful misfortune.

Missing Childhood

I've read about people missing their childhood.
Like it was a time,
Where everything was so much simpler.
A time when the world wasn't so dark and mean.
A place they were loved for just existing.

I can't relate to that,
But it sounds nice.
Few years of childhood innocence,
A time of just being,
Taking shelter in blissful ignorance.

Before the real world wakes you up,
And the stress of life takes over,
How to be and what to do with yourself,
And why it's so difficult to manage?

I didn't get any of those easy years.
From the start,
I realized it wasn't great.
I thought that I would be better alone,
Without rules and control.
And constant stress of pleasing them.

I love you and it's not enough • Christa Kate Anderson

Except it wasn't and still isn't,
But I don't want my childhood back,
It still was worse than being an adult.
I'm just left with this feeling,
Of how much I missed out,
And didn't get to have.

Heartbreak

Let me go

It all started so fast as obsession,
Craving for more and more,
And you were there and I had my fix.
Your touch was fire and I let it burn.

Hoping that I will come out safe,
That it will not burn me alive.
How dare you say that you love me,
When you hate yourself?

Your problems turned into mine,
You pushed me away.
Then all you wanted was her.
I wasn't good enough, but why?

It killed a part of me,
But I still cared for you,
Why didn't you let me go?
You dragged me along.

I love you and it's not enough • Christa Kate Anderson

It hurt me more,
You cried in my arms,
And said you can't lose me.
Was it all a lie?

Then she left and you missed me,
And wanted back what we had.
We said we will give it a try,
But it wasn't the same.

The fire had turned into ice.
I couldn't breathe anymore,
And had nothing left for you,
But the power was finally mine.

Never enough

I tried so hard,
Gave you everything I had,
And was the best I could be.
Just to see you happy.

It was never enough,
As you wanted more and more.
How much do you need?

I'm always the one to take the blame,
You are never wrong,
And never sorry.

So cold and far when you're next to me.
When I say *I love you*,
You say *Thank you*.
Do you even care?

I was so stupid for loving you.
You look for the next best thing,
When you already have it all.

My heart is breaking.
You will never change,
And I have myself to blame.

The game

The game of power and control was so easy to play,
But I could never win.
Putting me down just to pick me up again.

My honesty was met with lies,
Care with more and more problems,
Always being my fault,
Saying those words and then making me suffer.

It was like a weapon against me.
I wasn't the one lying,
But that's what I got back.
The best of me wasn't close to being enough.
I was made to believe that the problem was me.

The day the switch flipped and I was done.
The last time I said it,
It was a lie.
It became unbearable,
And I was finally free.

Love and pain

When love equals pain,
And caring is the biggest crime,
The weakness that can't be allowed,
And people turn so cold.

I don't know who I am anymore,
All I really have is myself.
And all the thoughts inside.
But will it ever be enough?

Am I me when there is no You?
When there is no one around,
One wrong step will set you back,
And shut you out.

No one wants to feel the pain,
But we do want love,
As they go hand in hand,
There is not one without the other.

Was it worth having it for a bit,
Just to feel alive,
And then lose it in a heartbeat?
What is real and where is the lie?

But it's better to know you can feel,
That is the price you pay for being real,
As you close your mind and open your heart,
Hoping it will be worth it one day.

The idea of us

You and the idea of us,
Something I wanted so badly,
More than myself,
Losing it more with each day.
You asked me to forgive and forget.

You wanted me to be patient and kind,
To understand and care.
All for you and us,
And the future.
I had nothing left,
And you had nothing to give.

You asked me to trust you and lie,
I pushed back my thoughts.
You said that you know what's best.
But it was all for you,
Not me or us.

I love you and it's not enough • Christa Kate Anderson

Broken heart

It hurts and I can't fall asleep.
It feels heavy and it's difficult to breathe.
I beg for someone to stop this feeling.
Do you have any idea what you did to me?

It's over and done, and long gone,
But I'm still feeling the pain in my heart.
Why does it keep coming back?
I wish I could shut it off.

I'm happy and I get distracted,
Loving it when it goes away,
Until it comes back and I'm gasping for air,
And again I am back with the pain.

Is this normal or should I look for help?
I wish I could take a pill and make it go away.
Like getting rid of a headache.
Time goes and it doesn't get better.

I'm finding ways to distract myself more,
I'm thankful for the times without the pain,
I hate it when it comes back to me,
But I'm used to it by now and it's a part of me.

I love you and it's not enough • *Christa Kate Anderson*

Oh shit, no!

That *oh shit, no* moment, not again.
Here I am back at it.
Can I do this once more?
When I know how bad the end can be.

I'm terrified of feeling my world crashing,
Breaking down again in a moment's notice,
Just to force myself to get back up.

That was the worst and best thing for me,
I came out better.
And it showed me how deeply I can feel.
But it hurt like hell.

Piece by piece putting it back together,
And crying so hard I could barely breathe,
Screaming in silence from the top of my lungs.
And wishing I would disappear.

It's not in pieces, but it's not the same,
Sometimes it feels whole, but then it still hurts,
As the uneasy feeling takes over,
It echoes the pain from before.

What if

I had you for a little bit,
And then you were gone,
Taking all the what-ifs away.

I didn't get to hold you.
And I wonder,
How that would have been,
While I'm left with a hole instead.

As much as I loved you,
That wasn't enough.
And it took me by surprise,
When you had to die.

I am the one to blame,
And this is a cruel joke.
That's what he said,
When all I had left was *sorry*.

Could I have done something different,
To still have you here?
I'm sorry for the disappointment,
And that I wasn't good enough.

Throat infection

You're like a never-ending throat infection.
It hurts and it burns.
You make it impossible to breathe.
No amount of tea I drink helps to wash you away.

Just when I think it's over,
It's only another beginning of pain.
You just lay there inside of me,
And wait for your turn to make my life miserable again.

I can't shake you off.
You're like a tattoo after a drunken night out,
I never asked for it,
Never wanted it,
And now I'm stuck with it.

Reflections on love

I didn't treat any of them badly,
I have my default personality,
That is loving and caring by nature.
I just didn't care that much about them.

I wasn't that bothered about them being around me.
I do like my space and thought,
It was normal to feel like that.
It probably came from a more selfish perspective.
I was more concerned with what I can get out of them.

I didn't mean to do that,
I tried to please them,
Make them like me more and more,
Giving them more of myself.

You wouldn't say that it was acting selfish,
But it was.
It came from a place of insecurity.
Wanting approval and love from outside.
I needed something out of them,
God, it felt good to hear that they loved me!

I love you and it's not enough • *Christa Kate Anderson*

Someone did when I didn't.
I desperately needed to hear that,
They were lying but I didn't care.
I heard what I wanted and ignored the rest.
And you can't give what you don't have.

When I said I loved them it was a lie,
I didn't have that love for myself.
They didn't deserve my love.
No, I wasn't the best me to them,
But they weren't the best of themselves to me.

Two years and I didn't know him,
Or care to get to know him.
He was there because I needed someone to be there.
He needed someone to use,
And treat like shit while promising the world.

And after him,
I needed someone to help me forget and distract me,
To make it all better.
I needed him to feel safe,
Because I didn't have safety in me.
He needed someone to give him care and attention,
While he hated himself.

I love you and it's not enough • *Christa Kate Anderson*

This is what love,
And loving someone doesn't look like.
I didn't know any better at that time.

Coming out of it,
I found the real me.
Everything I need for myself,
I finally have everything to give,
I have that in myself.
And now it's sharing that.

ACKNOWLEDGEMENTS

This wouldn't be happening without the love and support
of my partner, who's read all of my poems and helped with
making this book.
In the neverending crowd of crappy people and families,
he's the one thing that I got right.

ABOUT THE AUTHOR

Christa loves to write about society, people and feelings that come as part of the human experience. She likes being in nature and taking photos of beautiful things.
This is her first self-published poetry collection.

She can be found on Instagram @ChristaKateAnderson

And on her blog: Society Through the Lens of a Poet

Find her on Instagram

@CHRISTAKATEANDERSON

Sharing with credit is
welcome.

THANK YOU FOR
READING.

I hope you enjoyed reading my poems, let me know if
anything made you feel something or if you could relate to
anything in them.
I would love to hear about that.

If you could leave a review and let me know what you think on
Amazon or Goodreads, that would be so helpful. Thank you.

Christa K. Anderson

Printed in Great Britain
by Amazon

24352154R00079